# Someone Else's Earth

*poems by*

# Margaret Lee

*Finishing Line Press*
Georgetown, Kentucky

# Someone Else's Earth

Copyright © 2021 by Margaret Lee
ISBN 978-1-64662-608-3 First Edition
All rights reserved under International and Pan-American Copyright Conventions. No part of this book may be reproduced in any manner whatsoever without written permission from the publisher, except in the case of brief quotations embodied in critical articles and reviews.

## ACKNOWLEDGMENTS

This is my debut poetry collection, containing previously unpublished poems. I send special thanks to Katherine Miller, in whose high school classroom my love for the humanities was born; to the late Ivy Dempsey, poet and friend, who first thought that I "might like to make poems," to Judy Dearborn Nill, who reads and listens like no one else, and to Brandon Scott, who urged me to translate Sappho's fragments myself.

Publisher: Leah Huete de Maines
Editor: Christen Kincaid
Cover Art: Margaret Lee
Author Photo: Bernard Brandon Scott
Cover Design: Elizabeth Maines McCleavy

Order online: www.finishinglinepress.com
also available on amazon.com

Author inquiries and mail orders:
Finishing Line Press
PO Box 1626
Georgetown, Kentucky 40324
USA

# Table of Contents

Reflections ........................................................................... 1

Insight .................................................................................. 2

Dreamscape ....................................................................... 3

Quarantine ......................................................................... 4

Reverberations .................................................................. 5

Outer Space, Inner Light ................................................ 6

Visitors Unwelcome ........................................................ 8

Obsession ........................................................................... 9

This Web of Days ........................................................... 10

Earthbound ...................................................................... 12

Reflections on a Cancer Diagnosis ............................. 14

Intensity ............................................................................ 15

Worry-cloud .................................................................... 16

Clover Dance ................................................................... 17

Relentless as the Sea ...................................................... 19

Desert Yearning .............................................................. 20

Consuming Tide ............................................................. 22

Weighted, Waiting .......................................................... 23

The Damask of Our Days ............................................. 25

Hope .................................................................................. 27

*For KCM,
friend and beloved teacher
who introduced me to Sappho
and the ancient world*

## About the Poems

These poems were inspired by the extant fragments of the lyric poet Sappho (c. 630 - c. 570 BCE), an ancient voice who sang a woman's songs from an island and endured. Of the 10,000 lines Sappho may have written, about 650 survive. Just one of Sappho's surviving poems is complete. We possess only fragments of her other poems.

Sappho's whispers tantalize. Her songs, incomplete, entreat the missing verses and refrains. For this chapbook, I selected twenty Sappho fragments and translated them into English from the Greek text at https://digitalsappho.org/title-page/. I then built new poems around these fragmentary remains. My poems do not and cannot restore Sappho's words or intentions. Instead, I fill the gaps with shards of my own experience.

I show my translation of each Sappho fragment in italics at the top of a new page. My poem appears below the translated fragment that inspired it. Words from the Sappho fragment that appear in my poem are shown in italics.

Sappho's fragments have fascinated scholars and poets for more than two millennia. We cannot reconstitute her work but we can celebrate her enduring eloquence. Sappho has seduced me into poetry writing. She sings on, with a chorus of voices old and new.

# Reflections

Fragment 4
*thirst for purpose*
*wholly*
*I can*
*]*
*if I could*
*to reflect*
*face*
*]*
*touched*
*]*

Though I see death's shadow, *a thirst for purpose* wells up,
an emptiness consuming more *wholly* than fear.
    Breathing in, *I can* feel its advancing boundary.
    Breathing out, I reach for what I cannot yet see.
Actually slaking that thirst, even *if I could*, would go too far—
impossible for any bounded thing *to reflect* this search.
    Yearning molds a lovely *face*, glowing with conviction,
    but satisfaction caps the well of emptiness within.
My face, touched by time's march,
    still registers my thirst,
    still draws from that well of emptiness.

**Insight**

Fragment 12
]
]
]
*thought*
]
]
]
]
]

A creaking hinge,
then pale light
the moment
a fresh *thought* dawns.
Insight steps
through the clutter
like a child
moving through the house
when no one else is awake.

# Dreamscape

Fragment 24C
]
*we live*
]
*opposite*
]
*courage*
*man*
]
]

In a dream I envisioned the place
where we *live* as a great house with no one in charge
and a madman loose inside.
A strange source delivered protection—
  the *opposite* of waking reality.
In a corner stood a benevolent but impotent authority
  (that part was real)
who drew a gun on the madman and shot.
  Somehow I found *courage*
to command the *man* to yield.
I pointed a larger gun and demanded,
"Put it down."
He did.
And the madman, too,
succumbed.

**Quarantine**

Fragment 24D
*bottom*
*]*
*]*
*]*
*]*
*in faint cries*
*]*

At the *bottom* of isolation
the days pile up like dirty laundry.
Their edges dissolve into the expanding heap—
time no longer marks them until
innate rhythms peck from inside their shells.
Then, *in faint cries,*
they speak.

## Reverberations

Fragment 29A
*]*
*]*
*depths*
*]*

That place within,
sheltered by inner parts,
attuned to seismic *depths*,
knows my strength, my flaws, my fate.

## Outer Space, Inner Light

Fragment 34
*stars around the lovely moon*
*hold back their brilliant shape*
*when she shines full*
*… earth*
*]*
*silver*

How little we see
of what lies before us.
Landscape, neighborhood,
emotional terrain
hide in plain sight,
exposed but invisible.
Even *stars around the lovely moon*
*hold back their brilliant shape*
when she shines *full*
on the *earth*,
itself cloaked in darkness
except for those few features
revealed but distorted
under her *silver* gleam.

We are ever
someone else's earth,
concealed
except for those few features
another light relumes,
as if there could be
        only one light,
        one star,
        one focal point.

Is not the moon's glow itself a reflection
of the sun's violent boil,
our system's brilliant core?
The mere, mean earth
seems to extinguish the moon's radiance
when she turns her face away.
And does not the moon ride in earth's orbit,
dependent on her enraptured gaze?
And what of other galaxies,
evident only as eclipses, anomalies—
distant and unseen
except for those few features
that distort our perception
of the night sky?

To face the light—
to step out from behind
the earth and its moon,
those obstacles twice and three times
removed from the really real—
such a turn would unhide
our true forms,
their luminous contours,
except for those few features
that we share in common
with all that is.

It would ignite the stars,
reveal new constellations
in the night sky.

## Visitors Unwelcome

Fragment 42
*their frenzy cooled*
*they lowered their wings*

Torturous thoughts,
dread of catastrophes not yet real
but impending—
these are the howling harpies
of the mind,
sweeping the storm winds,
provoking terror.

I sensed the moment
when *their frenzy cooled.*
They lowered their wings—
a hush ran ahead,
a pressure lifted.
My breath returned.

**Obsession**

Fragment 48
*you came and I was eager for you
you cooled my inner parts that burned with yearning*

Unbidden, *you came
and I was eager for you*
like a bee swarm in a clover field,
fragrant, alive!

Unfaltering, I fixed my gaze.
*You cooled my inner parts that burned with yearning,*
one breath from despair.
Now one breath inspires our shared life.

## This Web of Days

Fragment 51
*I do not know where to run*
*in me two ways of thinking*

*I do not know where to run—*
*in me, two ways of thinking*
materialize, then dissolve,
each in its turn,
until I wonder whether
they are just the same—
living,
dying.

Decisions unravel
       and the broken ends fray,
the day's torn garment
unmended.
What would I change
       if I knew for sure
that today was the end?
Could I make it any better?
Could it be any worse?
What of tomorrow?
More to dread? to regret?

Only the living
tear their clothes in grief.
The dead lie motionless
beneath their shrouds.

Destiny's taut warp strands interlace
with the weft of intention,
always under tension.
Thus our will and our fate
hold us in place—
life's integral fabric
shot through with color,
rippling with each day's textures,
soon to be cut from the loom.

We are just this—
        this tension,
        this web of days
straining against each other,
held together
by all that threatens
to tear us apart.

## Earthbound

Fragment 52
*I would not think fit to touch the sky*

In the fir forest
the floor tilts and boundaries melt.
Everything clings to something else—
      the mossy drape,
      walls of fern,
      lichens etched in basalt—
all seek stability in misty gloom,
surreal in dark monochrome,
a million shades of green.

Nothing dares to reach for distant heavens
inside this green-grown world
      where forest features twist and roil
      with the bend and bevel of the earth,
their edges indistinguishable from their shadows,
a dreamscape's convolution—
      eerie, imposing.

I, too, hug the earth
amid mushrooms half-hidden in peaty turf—
      bizarre shapes, invisibly entwined
      with tree roots buried deep.
*I would not think fit to touch the sky*
where rocks and roots grasp handholds
      to keep from falling—
      silent, invisible.

Only rainy rivulets
glistening down basalt cliffs
willingly yield to gravitation,
hushed and sparkling,
seeking their level,
down, down,
        against the earth,
        into the earth.
I resist the slide,
unwilling to disappear
like rainwater
        against the earth,
        inside the earth.

## Reflections on a Cancer Diagnosis

Fragment 67A
*]*
*and this*
*deadly god*
*truly I did not love*
*now, though, because*
*and the cause neither*
*nothing much*
*]*

Life-dreams, slowly shackled by learned fears,
the accretions of a lifetime,

choked quiet in the grip of recent wounds—
reverses, inadvertencies, years of disappointment—

and *this* lethal intrusion now from some
*deadly god* run amok—this I resisted.

*Truly, I did not love fantasy* or luxury then.
*Now, though, because* death lurks, I lust—

*and the cause neither* vengeful nor desperate—
*nothing much* beyond life's own breath

in my nostrils, innocent.

**Intensity**

Fragment 85B
*]*
*like an old man*
*]*

He studied the bug in his jar,
squinting *like an old man*
loving truth more than life.

**Worry-cloud**

Fragment 87B
*anxiety*
*land*
*]*
*]*

Anxiety, infectious fog,
hovers over the *land* and recoils,
impotent to choke
her earthy fragrances—verdant, stony.

**Clover Dance**

Fragment 125
*I used to braid coronets*

*I used to braid coronets*
from long-stemmed sweet clover
grown wild and tall in the late-summer lawn,
when the mowers finally admitted defeat
        after trying in vain
        to contain sun-rich Bermuda
        within its concrete boundaries.
Better by far, I thought, the soft, shaggy grass tips
        of neglected turf
        than a prickly green surface
        mown flat and laced with gasoline fumes.

And best of all, the white clover blossoms,
        drawing honeybees with their scent
        and sporting those strange composite flowers—
            clusters of tiny trumpets,
        upturned in the flower-head's center,
        downturned around the edge.

Sometimes a few cornets blush pink
        where the blossoms meet their sepals,
        a modest display of summer's extravagance.
Those are the ones you could pluck
        with delicate, little-girl fingers
        and gently bite the tiny tube's rosy base
        with your front teeth,
        just partway through.
Then a quick, sweet flush
        would waft past your nose and tongue.
Bite too hard and it's bitter,
        or tastes like nothing at all.

Those clover garlands encircling my head
dissolved the cement circumference
       of our yard,
       our family,
as if its slender stems would never snap.

My flowery diadems enclosed another, unbounded world.
There I was more than myself.
I was also my dreams,
       my drawings,
       my construction-paper crafts,
       the colored pebbles I collected,
       my stashed-away secrets,
       my prayers,
       my scribbled hopes—
the self I never showed anyone.
Because, why? She wasn't real.

Yet she moved, breathed
       and danced
              when ringed with clover.

## Relentless as the Sea

Fragment 145
*do not churn gravel*

Numinous, the ocean captivates,
    neither kind nor cruel
    but indifferent.
Waves *do not churn gravel* with intention.
The surf tosses rocks where it will—
random, irresistible.

Relentless, its watery churn,
    moving and mixing
    mollusk and kelp
in a salty slurry
along with their dead remains,
blurring the distinction.

Riveted, I search its constant heaving,
    drawn like the tide
    by otherworldly forces
to find meaning, inscribe purpose,
my breath's oscillation
relentless as the sea.

## Desert Yearning

Fragment 146
*neither the honey nor the bee for me*

*Neither the honey nor the bee, for me.*
None of its industry,
its tireless devotion to the task,
the hive's countless mazes,
tiny compartments,
and a queen at the center—
        silent, invisible.

No hopeful buzzing, pregnant
with the promise of sticky sweet
amber liquid dripping from the comb.
No soft, waxy protective layer securing its treasure.
No golden excess, gluing honeyed cells together,
enticing the desire
        for more, more.

No. Abandon me to the desert
among the chamisa and sage
where only ants and armored beetles crawl,
where lizards skitter from shadows among the rocks.
Only wind traffic across the plateau—
        sometimes subtle,
        sometimes rumbling with pressure,
        always endless—
no beginning, no destination—
the earth's breath undulating with change,
the coming and going of days,
        retreating summer,
        advancing winter,
        spasms of storm.

Let there be moonlight,
always in motion—
> first its glow from behind mountain peaks,
> then bright beams across the steppe,
casting shadows—
flashlights exposing, then eclipsing
every minor mound,
each tiny crack,
making the arroyos yawn, gape,
then disappear—
proof that the desert remains,
> even in the dark,
> even at the mountains' feet,
> even under my feet.

The desert remains,
though its rocky plates heave and split,
and ancient lava, now stony and cool,
entombs its plains.
Exposed edges crumble grain by grain,
yielding to wind and weight,
rare rivers and flash floods.
Yet the surface holds,
> supports slender grasses, hairy arachnids,
> shelters rabbit and raven
> as they patrol the earth and sky.

Sometimes the desert carves a cliff face,
surrenders an aster's bloom,
pale purple against silver scrub,
or some other lovely thing.
Lovely or not,
it remains,
arid and spare—
> root-space here,
> crawl-places there—
a dry expanse reflecting
the moonlight.

## Consuming Tide

Fragment 167
*far whiter than an egg*

The sea's cold cuisine
frosts bulbous basalt mounds
with its saline meringue,
*far whiter than an egg*
and equally albuminous,
rich with jelly fragments
and debris from shells scraped clean,
then whipped to a froth
and piped in squiggly lines
along the rocky shore—
a fleeting visual confection
swallowed by the next wave.

## Weighted, Waiting

Fragment 168C
*the earth, many-crowned*
*in colored embroidery*

*The earth, many-crowned*
*in colored embroidery*
wears her cloaks of concrete, glass and steel.
The glistening spires of city skylines
adorn creeping urban sprawls,
        revise her contours.
Factories festoon her river valleys.
Shipping cranes bedeck her harbors.
Power plants, shimmering with light,
        encrust the plains.

But now, in the throes
of global pandemic,
jeweled towers stand idle.
The refinery's flare flashes and fades.
The jet stream meanders its course,
        unencumbered now by smog.

Her weighty spangles a burden now,
the earth sighs,
settles into the quiet,
takes stock of wounded humanity,
        awaiting our next move.

We wait, too,
sequestered in our beehives,
for the plague to pass.
Gradually our frenzy abates.
The ringing in our ears
        subsides.

As the quiet settles in,
our senses awaken
to the earth's movements—
      her daily rotation,
      her breath's gentle heaving,
      her lifeblood coursing through rivers and streams.
We can hear her heartbeat.
      We listen.

## The Damask of Our Days

Fragment 188
*epic-weaver*

Sing, O Voice within,
who hears melodies
where others find only broken threads,
their colors faded,
their integrity long lost
to some violent event
or the quiet wear and tear of
passing days.

These severed strands seem damaged
only when seen
for their original purpose,
their song choked out,
their refrain unsung.

When seen
just as they are,
interlaced so far and no farther,
with split seams and edges unraveling,
they become the wooly weft
of life's tapestry,
discontinuous,
leaving space for new silken strands,
for subtle colors.

These yarns were spun
to curl and twist,
dart and hide—
no plan from the distaff,
no chart for these threads,
random notes on separate staves.

Yet they find their way,
O, *Epic-weaver*,
when you give them voice,
come harmony, counterpoint, cacophony—
grand adventures,
heroic feats,
tempestuous loves
        with fervent intentions
        and tragic desires,
colossal miscalculations,
epic journeys in unknown lands—
the damask of our days.

The story is all.
So don your cloak
and sing their songs!
Make it sweet, noble,
something to live for,
something to die for.
Weave it well
with color and light.
Tell it true.

**Hope**

Fragment 191
*celery*

Again the persistent Perhaps
sends up green shoots,
tall and slender,
pale and fine,
like *celery*
sucking water from the earth,
resisting life's crunch
with stringy threads of resolve.

Margaret Lee is retired as Assistant Professor of Humanities at Tulsa Community College in Tulsa, Oklahoma. She attended Edgecliff College in Cincinnati, Ohio and graduated with a Bachelor of Arts in History from Seattle University in Seattle, Washington. She received a Master of Divinity from Phillips Theological Seminary in Tulsa, Oklahoma, and a Doctor of Theology from the Melbourne College of Divinity in Melbourne, Australia. Her doctoral dissertation, *A Method for Sound Analysis in Hellenistic Greek*, proposes a process for analyzing ancient Greek literature as speech. She is the editor of *Sound Matters: New Testament Studies in Sound Mapping* (Eugene, OR: Wipf and Stock, 2018) and is co-author with Bernard Brandon Scott of *Sound Mapping the New Testament* (Salem, OR: Polebridge Press, 2009). Margaret has written numerous articles on the Greek language and New Testament studies in edited books and peer-reviewed academic journals.

Before teaching the Humanities to undergraduates, Margaret spent six years working in the finance industry in Seattle, Washington, then twenty-five years in higher education administration in Tulsa, Oklahoma. She raised her daughter and son in Tulsa and now has three grandchildren. Margaret avidly pursues the fiber arts, including spinning, weaving, and knitting. Margaret enjoys sketching with pencil, ink, and watercolor. She is an enthusiastic birdwatcher and aspiring naturalist. Margaret loves exploring the Oklahoma prairies, New Mexico deserts, and Oregon coastal forests and seashores. She is a member of the Society of Biblical Literature, a fellow of the Westar Institute, an officer of the Tulsa Handspinner's Guild, and past president of the Tulsa Handweavers Guild. Margaret is a member of the Tulsa NightWriters, the Oklahoma Writers Federation, Inc., the Society of the Muse of the Southwest (SOMOS), and the Academy of American Poets.

www.ingramcontent.com/pod-product-compliance
Lightning Source LLC
LaVergne TN
LVHW041508070426
835507LV00012B/1420